How Things Work

Library Edition Published 1990

Published by Marshall Cavendish Corporation
147 West Merrick Road
Freeport, Long Island
N.Y. 11520

Printed in Italy by New Interlitho, Milan

© Marshall Cavendish Limited 1989
© Cherrytree Press Limited 1988

Library Edition produced by DPM Services Limited

Library of Congress Cataloging-in-Publication Data

Kerrod, Robin.
    How things work / by Robin Kerrod: illustrated by Mike Atkinson and Sarah Atkinson.
      p. cm. — (Secrets of science : 3)
    "A Cherrytree book."
    Includes index
    Summary: Projects, activities, and experiments explore such areas of technology as the wheel, rocket power, kite flying, and magnetism.
    1. Scientific recreations — Juvenile literature. 2. Technology - Juvenile literature. [1. Scientific recreations. 2. Technology.]
    I. Atkinson, Mike. [1]. II. Atkinson, Sarah, [1]. III. Title.
  IV. Series: Kerrod, Robin, Secrets of science : 3.
    Q164.K46 1989
    530'.078 — dc19   89-918
                                      CIP
                                       AC

ISBN 1-85435-154-0
ISBN 1-85435-151-6(set)

SECRETS OF SCIENCE

How Things Work

Robin Kerrod

Illustrated by Mike Atkinson
and Sarah Atkinson

MARSHALL CAVENDISH
NEW YORK · LONDON · TORONTO · SYDNEY

Safety First

☐ Ask an adult for permission before you start any experiment, especially if you are using matches or anything hot, sharp, or poisonous.

☐ Don't wear good clothes. Wear old ones or an apron.

☐ If you work on a table, use an old one and protect it with paper or cardboard.

☐ Do water experiments in the sink, on the draining board, or outdoors.

☐ Strike matches away from your body, and make sure they are out before you throw them away.

☐ Make sure candles are standing securely.

☐ Wear oven gloves when handling anything hot.

☐ Be careful when cutting things. Always cut away from your body.

☐ Don't use tin cans with jagged edges. Use those with lids.

☐ Use only safe children's glue, glue sticks, or paste.

☐ **Never** taste chemicals, unless the book tells you to.

☐ Label all bottles and jars containing chemicals, and store them where young children can't get at them – and never in the family's food cupboard.

☐ Never use or play with electricity. It can KILL. Use a battery to create a current if needed.

☐ When you have finished an experiment, put your things away, clean up, and wash your hands.

Contents

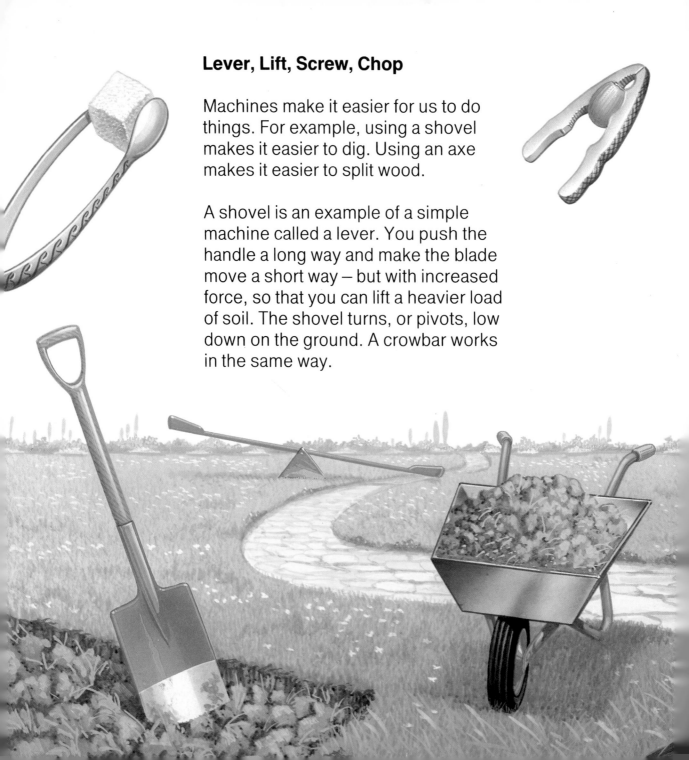

Lever, Lift, Screw, Chop

Machines make it easier for us to do things. For example, using a shovel makes it easier to dig. Using an axe makes it easier to split wood.

A shovel is an example of a simple machine called a lever. You push the handle a long way and make the blade move a short way – but with increased force, so that you can lift a heavier load of soil. The shovel turns, or pivots, low down on the ground. A crowbar works in the same way.

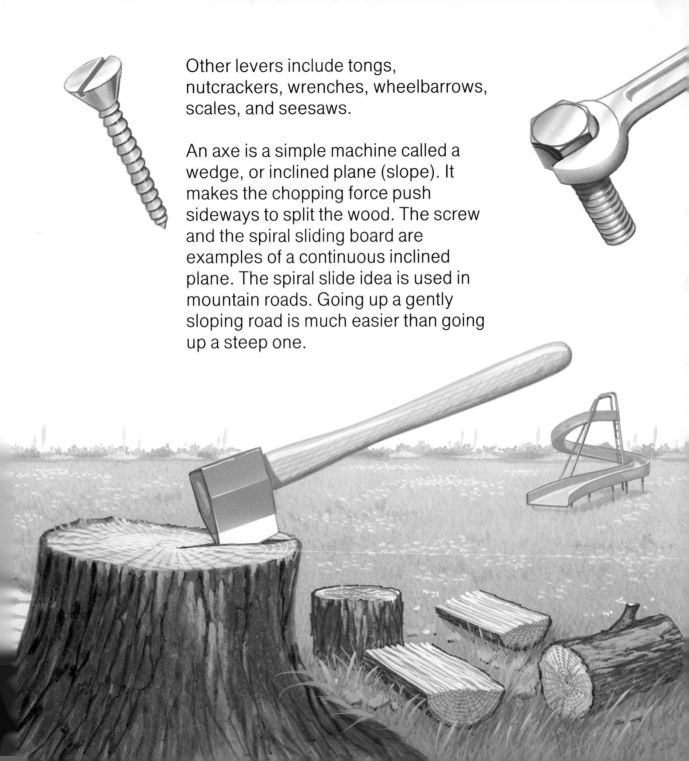

Other levers include tongs, nutcrackers, wrenches, wheelbarrows, scales, and seesaws.

An axe is a simple machine called a wedge, or inclined plane (slope). It makes the chopping force push sideways to split the wood. The screw and the spiral sliding board are examples of a continuous inclined plane. The spiral slide idea is used in mountain roads. Going up a gently sloping road is much easier than going up a steep one.

Wheels at Work

The most important simple machine of all is the wheel. When things move, they rub against each other. This rubbing is called friction, and it slows things down. Wheels make things move more easily because they reduce friction.

Try pushing a heavy load, such as a pile of bricks, along the ground. It's difficult, isn't it? Put the bricks on top of a row of pencils, and see how easily they move. The pencils roll like little wheels, and lower the friction with the ground.

Gears are wheels with teeth around the outside. The teeth of two gears lock together so that one turns the other. When they are different sizes, they turn at different speeds. There are lots of little gear wheels inside ordinary clocks and watches. They drive the hour and minute hands at different speeds.

A Spool Roller

1 You need a spool, a rubber band, two matchsticks, and tape.

2 Thread the rubber band through the hole in the spool and anchor it at one end with a matchstick and tape.

3 Put another matchstick through the rubber band at the other end, and wind it round and round.

4 Place the spool on the ground, let go, and watch it roll.

Reel It Up

A pulley makes it easier to lift heavy loads. It has one or more wheels with ropes passing over them. You can make a pulley using spools.

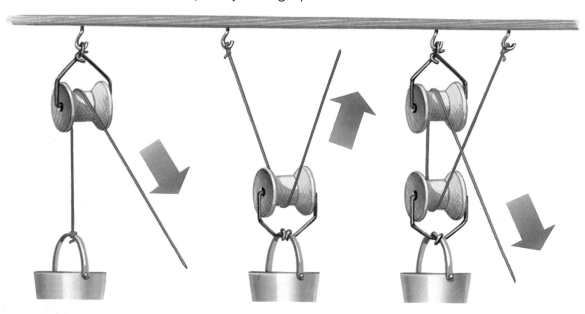

Make a Pulley

1 You need two spools, four screw hooks, some stiff but bendable wire, some string, a heavy load such as a toy bucket full of sand, a wooden bar or shelf to hang your pulleys from, and permission to use it!

2 Screw four hooks into the wood.

3 Thread a loop of wire through a spool, knot it firmly, and hang it from the first hook. This is a pulley.

4 Tie one end of a piece of string to your load, and put the other over the spool. Pull on the string, and see how easily it lifts.

5 Now, make another pulley, and this time attach it to the load.

6 Attach one end of a piece of string to your second hook, loop it through the pulley, and pull. Is it easier to lift the load?

7 Take both of the pulleys you have made and use them together. Tie the string to the fourth hook, then loop it first through the pulley attached to the load, and then through a pulley attached to the third hook.

8 Now, pull on the string, and see how much lighter your load seems this time.

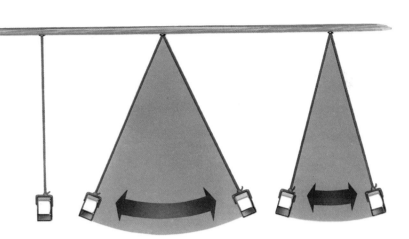

In the Swing

How long is a second? You could say it is 33 inches. See why. Tie a heavy iron nut to the end of a piece of thread at least 36 inches long. Hang it so that the thread is 33 inches long. Pull the nut to one side and let it swing. You have made a pendulum.

Using your watch, count how many times your pendulum swings in one minute. Back and forth counts as two swings. You will find that your pendulum makes about 60 swings, so each swing takes about a second. Grandfather clocks often have a pendulum with a one-second swing. That is why they are so tall.

Go Fly a Kite

A kite is a simple flying craft. It works in much the same way as a plane's wing. When it travels at an angle through the air, it rises because of a force pushing up on it, called lift.

Make a Kite

1 You need two wooden sticks about 32 inches long, string, tissue or crepe paper, glue or tape.

2 Lash the sticks together to make a cross, with one stick about 6 inches from the top of the other.

3 Notch the ends of the sticks, and tie string around the outside to make a kite shape.

4 Place the kite skeleton on the paper and cut out the kite, leaving an overlap of an inch at the edge.

5 Fold the paper over the string all the way around, and stick it in place with glue or tape.

6 Make a tail of folded paper tied to a string.

7 Cut a piece of string long enough to tie one end to the top of the kite and the other about two-thirds of the way down. This is the bridle. Notch the stick to keep it in place.

8 Tie a really long string about halfway along the bridle. Then wait for a breezy day, and give your kite a test flight.

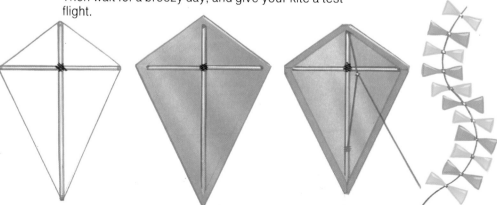

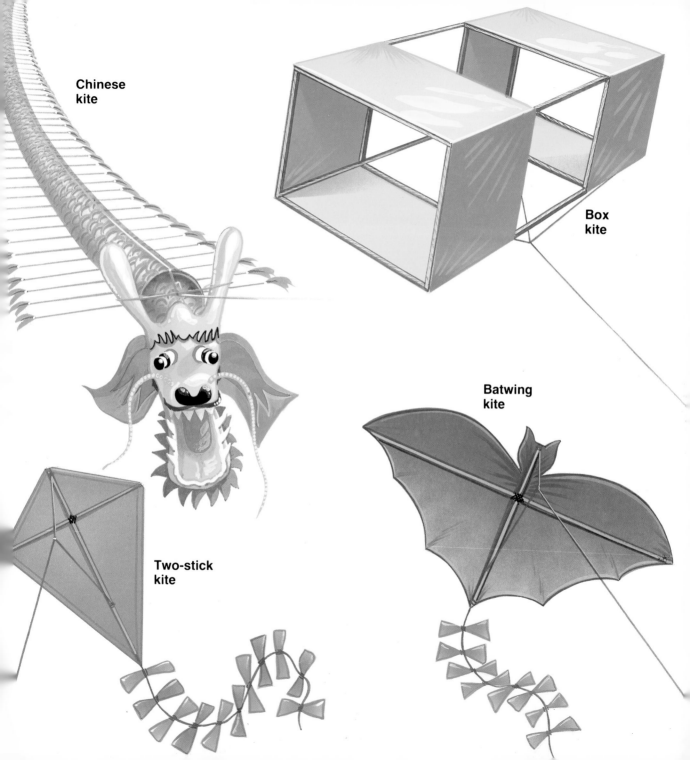

Chinese kite

Box kite

Batwing kite

Two-stick kite

Jet Set

Blow up a balloon, pinch the neck, and let it go. See how fast it flies through the air. It is traveling by jet propulsion, just as an airplane does. The air inside is rushing out in a jet. As the jet of air rushes backward, the balloon shoots forward. This effect is called **reaction**.

Reacting Bottle

1 You need scales, a bottle with a cork, some vinegar, and some baking powder.

2 Fill the bottle half full of water.

3 Add a little vinegar and a spoonful of baking powder to the bottle and quickly cork it.

4 Place it on the scale and stand back. (The cork will fly out of the bottle.)

5 Watch the scale as the cork shoots out. The bottle will be forced down in the opposite direction – by reaction.

14

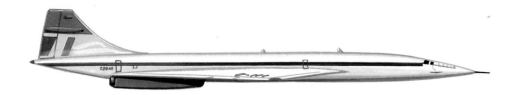

An aircraft jet engine burns fuel to make gases that shoot out backward. As they shoot backward, they push the aircraft forward, by reaction.

Inside the engine, the gases spin turbine wheels before escaping. That is why jets are sometimes called gas-turbine engines. You can make a turbine for yourself.

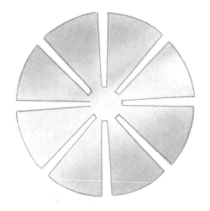

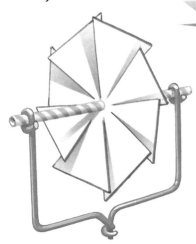

A Turbine Spinner

1 You need a piece of cardboard, a straw, and wire.

2 Cut a disk of cardboard, and make a hole in the center for the straw to go through.

3 Now cut evenly-spaced wedges to within ¼ inch of the center hole.

4 Bend each of the "blades" of the disk in the same direction.

5 Put the straw through the hole and attach it to a loop of wire fixed to its ends.

6 Blow on the wheel and see how your turbine spins.

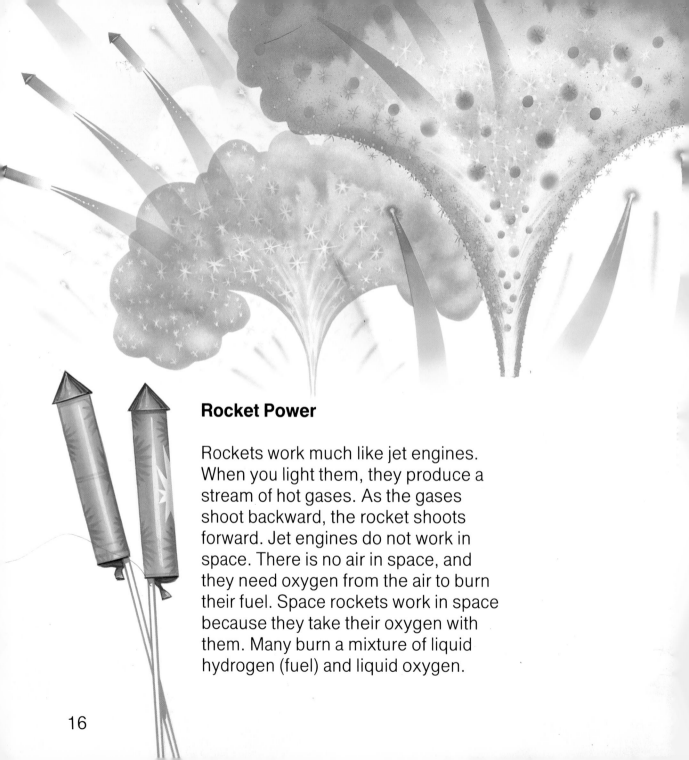

Rocket Power

Rockets work much like jet engines. When you light them, they produce a stream of hot gases. As the gases shoot backward, the rocket shoots forward. Jet engines do not work in space. There is no air in space, and they need oxygen from the air to burn their fuel. Space rockets work in space because they take their oxygen with them. Many burn a mixture of liquid hydrogen (fuel) and liquid oxygen.

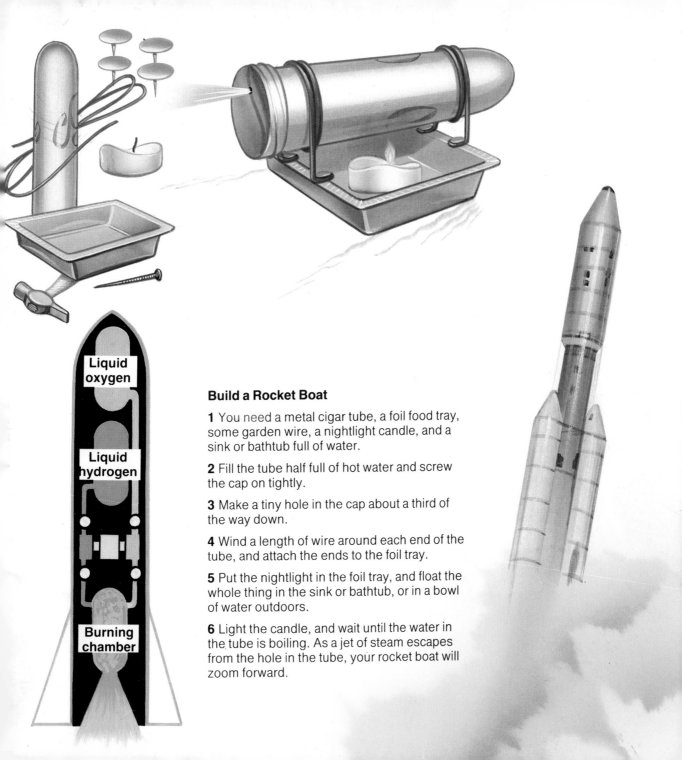

Build a Rocket Boat

1 You need a metal cigar tube, a foil food tray, some garden wire, a nightlight candle, and a sink or bathtub full of water.

2 Fill the tube half full of hot water and screw the cap on tightly.

3 Make a tiny hole in the cap about a third of the way down.

4 Wind a length of wire around each end of the tube, and attach the ends to the foil tray.

5 Put the nightlight in the foil tray, and float the whole thing in the sink or bathtub, or in a bowl of water outdoors.

6 Light the candle, and wait until the water in the tube is boiling. As a jet of steam escapes from the hole in the tube, your rocket boat will zoom forward.

Liquid oxygen

Liquid hydrogen

Burning chamber

Through a Pinhole

Photography – taking pictures with a camera – is the world's most popular hobby. A camera is basically very simple. It is a box with a hole in one end. The box contains a film which is sensitive to light. When the hole in the box is closed, it is completely dark inside. When it is opened, light rays fall on the film and make a picture. Try making this camera.

A Camera Obscura

1 You need a cardboard tube about 6 inches long, some black cardboard, parchment paper, black tape, a pin, and a sunny day.

2 Cut a disk of cardboard to fit over one end of the tube and make a tiny pinhole in the middle.

3 Tape the disk to the tube with black tape.

4 Tape a piece of parchment paper over the other end.

5 On a sunny day, close the curtains so that it is dark inside. Carefully let light into the pinhole end of the tube.

6 Look at the parchment paper; you will see an image of the scene outside. Don't be surprised – it will be upside down, because of the way light travels.

7 The device you have made is called a *camera obscura*. Years ago, artists used them when they made sketches.

18

The *camera obscura* focuses a picture on its screen, but you cannot keep a record of what you see. In cameras that contain film, you end up with a photograph. Cameras have a shutter over the hole to control how much light enters them, and they have a lens to focus the light. They can take very good pictures. See if you can take a good picture with this shoebox camera. It works with a pinhole.

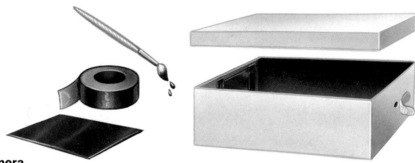

A Pinhole Camera

1 You need a shoe box, a pin, black paint, black tape, adhesive tape, a sheet of photographic film (which must not be exposed to light), a dark room, and someone to help.

2 Paint the inside of the box and its lid black.

3 Make a pinhole in the center of one end, and tape the adhesive tape over it.

4 Now switch the lights off, and make sure the room is absolutely dark. (See that you can lay hands on everything you need before you start. Two people working together will make this easier.)

5 In the dark, tape a piece of photographic film in the center of the inside wall of the box, directly opposite the pinhole. The dull side should face the pinhole.

6 Still working in the dark, put the lid on the box, and tape around it. Your camera is now ready.

7 Place the camera on a table with the pinhole facing the window. Being careful not to move the box, peel off the adhesive tape, and leave the camera for about 15 minutes.

8 Re-stick the tape. Then, again in the dark, remove the film and put it back in its envelope. Take it to be developed and printed.

Sounds Fun

You can have a "wail" of a time making music with homemade instruments. An old favorite is the comb and paper. The air vibrates between the comb and paper and produces a buzzing sound. But you couldn't call it music!

You can make an even worse noise with a ruler tied to the end of a piece of string. Twirl the ruler in the air (making sure nobody is in the way), and listen to the weird hums, wails, and howls that it makes. Pretend there is a storm and your ruler is the wind.

Pan pipes are a set of pipes of different lengths. Each one makes a noise with a different pitch, so that you really can make music. Make them with straws stuck to cardboard. You get sounds of varying pitch, too, if you blow over the necks of bottles partly filled with different amounts of water.

For a really brilliant sound, play the wine glasses. Fill wine glasses with different amounts of water. Lightly press a wet finger slowly round and round each rim. The glasses will give out beautiful pure notes.

It's For You-hoo

If you want to talk to a friend some distance away without everybody hearing, you can make this simple telephone. You don't have to pay for your calls on it!

Tin Telephone

1 You need two clean cans – the kind that have lids, about 25 yards of string, a hammer, and a nail.

2 Use the hammer and nail to make a hole in the middle of the bottom of each can.

3 Thread the ends of the string through the holes, and tie a large knot inside each can.

4 Give one can to your friend, and walk away from each other until the string is pulled taut. This is most important.

5 Signal your friend to start talking into his or her can, while you put your can to your ear.

6 You should be able to hear your friend quite well. His voice makes the bottom of his can vibrate. Then the twine carries the vibrations along the bottom of your can and makes that vibrate. Its vibrations set up sound waves, which you hear.

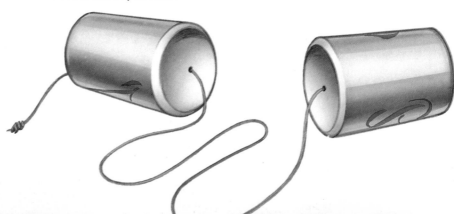

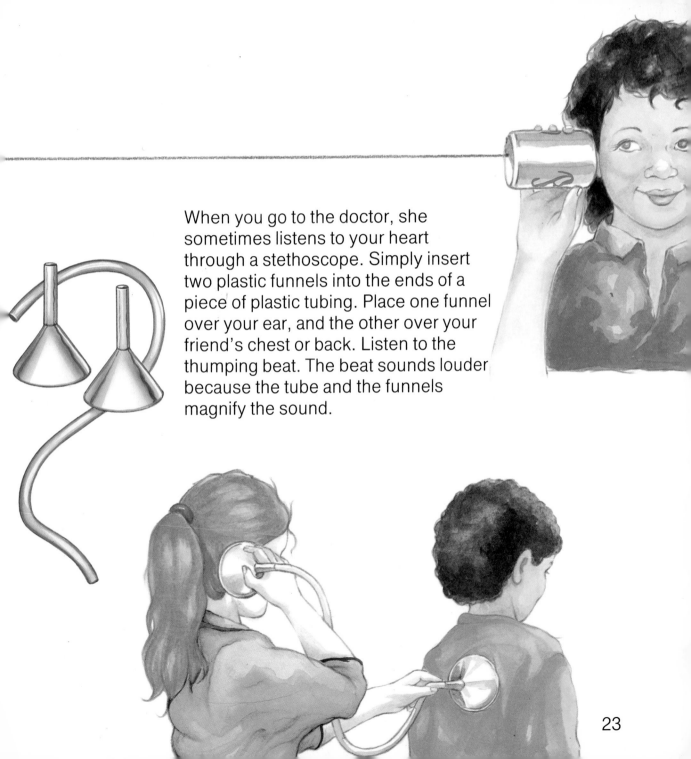

When you go to the doctor, she sometimes listens to your heart through a stethoscope. Simply insert two plastic funnels into the ends of a piece of plastic tubing. Place one funnel over your ear, and the other over your friend's chest or back. Listen to the thumping beat. The beat sounds louder because the tube and the funnels magnify the sound.

23

Flashing Messages

You can send a secret coded message to someone with this telegraph set. It uses flashing lights. If you want to send two-way messages, you will need two sets.

Telegraph Set

1 For each set, you need two small strips of tin (you can cut them from an old can, but if you do, ask an adult to help you. Thoroughly clean the metal and watch your fingers on the sharp edges); four thumbtacks; three lengths of copper wire (the lengths will depend on how far apart you want your sender and receiver to be, but 15 yards should be more than enough); a rectangular battery; a flashlight bulb; two flat blocks of wood; cardboard; sandpaper; an adult to help you.

Making the sender

2 Wind a length of copper wire around the shaft of a thumbtack, and then stick the tack in one of the blocks of wood (your base board) near the end.

3 Tap a hole for a thumbtack through the end of one of the tin strips.

4 Clean around the hole with sandpaper, and rub the other end of the strip with sandpaper until it is clean and shiny.

5 Wind one end of a length of copper wire around the shaft of another thumbtack, push it through the hole in the metal strip and into the base board. Position it so the other end of the strip lies over the first thumbtack.

Making the receiver

6 Cut a rectangle of cardboard about twice as wide as the metal strip, and make a hole in the middle – just big enough for the base of the lightbulb.

7 Push the base of the bulb and the third length of copper wire into the hole, so that the wire is touching the metal base of the bulb.

8 Cut out a strip of metal exactly like the one for the sender, with a hole for a thumbtack at each end.

9 Clean the tin strip with sand-paper, making sure that the middle is shiny clean. Tack it lightly to the second base board.

10 Take the other end of the wire that is attached to the tacked-down end of the sender's metal strip. Wind it around the shaft of a thumbtack, between the strip and the board.

11 Keeping the wire and the strip in position, ease out the tacks one at a time and tack the bulb-holder over the strip. The base of the bulb should touch the strip.

Making Contact

12 Attach the wire from the bulb to one side of the battery.

13 Attach the wire from the thumbtack under the sender strip to the other side of the battery.

14 Now everything is ready. The sender strip is a switch. When it makes contact with the thumbtack underneath, it completes an electrical circuit and should make the light on the receiver flash on.

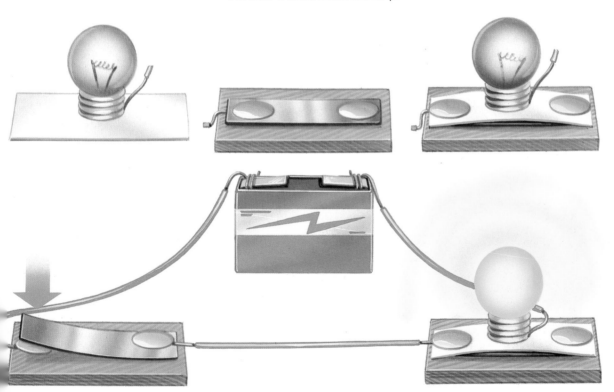

Which Way?

A magnet is a piece of iron or steel that attracts iron and other metals. Buy or borrow two small bar magnets. Hang them up on lengths of string, some distance from each other. What do you find? They both end up pointing in the same direction – north-south. Magnets always point north because they are being attracted by another big magnet – the earth itself. It is as if the earth has a huge magnet buried in it.

You can use a magnet to make a compass.

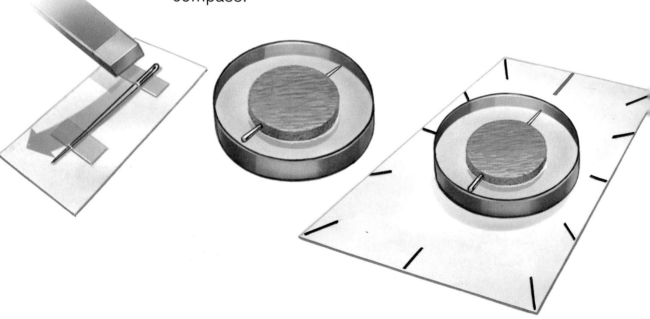

If you haven't got a compass, you can still tell directions – if you have a watch with hands. Point the hour hand at the sun. Then, take a line half way between the hour hand and 12 o'clock. That line points south.

Make a Compass

1 You need a metal lid, a piece of cardboard, a magnet (buy them in hobby shops), a cork, and a needle.

2 Tape the needle to the cardboard. Then stroke it about 50 times with one end of the magnet, always pulling in the same direction. Use the same end of the magnet, and lift it at the end of each stroke. By doing this, you make the needle into a little magnet. (Test it by picking up a pin with it.)

3 Push the needle through a thin slice of cork, and float the cork on water in the lid.

4 Draw a compass on the cardboard, showing the main points of the compass.

5 Place the magnetized needle in its holder on the cardboard. Make sure the two ends of the needle/magnet are pointing north and south on the card.

6 Check with the sun that your compass is correct. At noon, the sun lies in the south, and shadows point to the north.

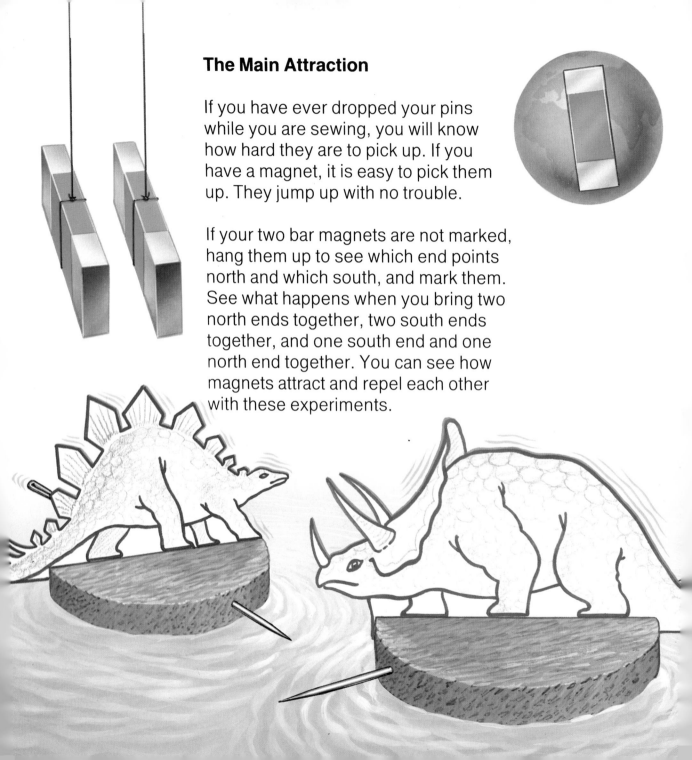

The Main Attraction

If you have ever dropped your pins while you are sewing, you will know how hard they are to pick up. If you have a magnet, it is easy to pick them up. They jump up with no trouble.

If your two bar magnets are not marked, hang them up to see which end points north and which south, and mark them. See what happens when you bring two north ends together, two south ends together, and one south end and one north end together. You can see how magnets attract and repel each other with these experiments.

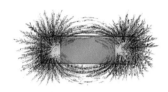

Fun with Filings

1 You need two magnets, cardboard, and some iron filings (tiny shavings of iron which you can buy with magnets).

2 Sprinkle some iron filings on your magnets. Notice how they cluster around the ends (poles).

3 Place the cardboard over one of the magnets and sprinkle some filings on top. Tap the cardboard, and notice the pattern that the filings form. This shows the magnetic field of the magnet.

Magnetic Monsters

1 You need two needles, a magnet, two flat corks, some thin cardboard, scissors, colored pens, and a sharp knife.

2 Magnetize the two needles by stroking them with a magnet (see page 26), and stick them through the corks.

3 Draw the most fearsome monsters you can on the cardboard, cut them out, and stand them in the cork (in a slit made carefully with the knife).

4 Put your monsters in a bowl of water and watch them jostle each other as the needle magnets push and pull.

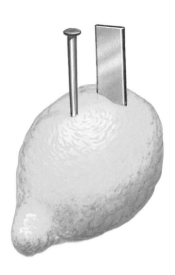

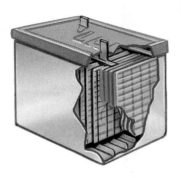

Electrifying Activity

Have you heard of an electric lemon?
Here is how to make one.

Electric Lemon

1 You need a soft, juicy lemon, a clean copper nail, and a sandpapered strip of zinc.

2 Stick the nail and the zinc strip into the lemon. Touch them lightly with your finger. Feel the tingle? Isn't it shocking? You have made a simple electric cell, or battery. It works by chemical action when the copper and zinc combine with the acid (juice) in the lemon.

See how electricity and magnetism go together. Set up the telegraph circuit shown on pages 24 and 25. Next to one of the wires, place the compass shown on page 26. Press the switch and see how the needle moves. This shows that a wire carrying an electric current becomes magnetic.

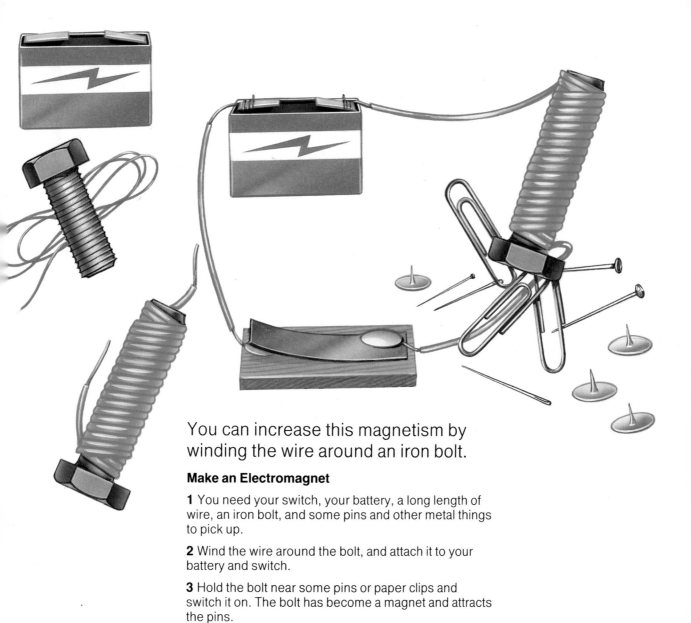

You can increase this magnetism by winding the wire around an iron bolt.

Make an Electromagnet

1 You need your switch, your battery, a long length of wire, an iron bolt, and some pins and other metal things to pick up.

2 Wind the wire around the bolt, and attach it to your battery and switch.

3 Hold the bolt near some pins or paper clips and switch it on. The bolt has become a magnet and attracts the pins.

4 Switch it off, and the pins fall away. The bolt has lost its magnetism. It is a temporary magnet, or electromagnet.

Index and Glossary